This coloring book belongs To

. . . .

Look on the bright side of life

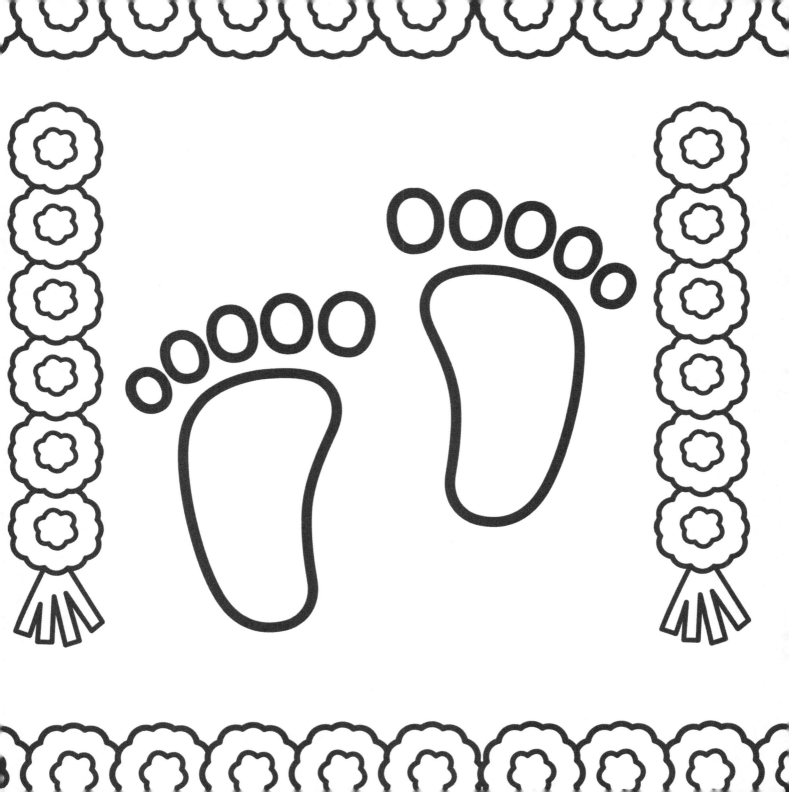

If you have enjoyed this coloring book, please leave a review.
It has a big impact on small businesses like us.
Thanks so much! :)

Made in the USA
Monee, IL
19 October 2024

68305090R00031